A Shared Vision

A Shared Vision

100 Exercises for Couples to Cocreate the Life of Their Dreams

Dr. Paulette Kouffman Sherman

Parachute Jump Publishing®

www.ParachuteJumpPublishing.com

ISBN 978-0-9852469-2-1

The mission of Parachute Jump Publishing:
Books that Inspire You to Love More

To couples everywhere
Who bring love to each other, to their
family, and to the world

Contents

Introduction

In my work with couples, I have noticed that many people get engaged and married without developing a shared vision. Each person is used to making decisions independently, and when they cohabitate they are shocked to discover that their partner has a different way of thinking, feeling, and living. Often this becomes a problem, so much so that over half of married couples eventually divorce. Many of them started out in love but never really took the time to get to know what their partner most needs. Sometimes partners do not even know what to discuss, so they remain silently in pain and can't begin to communicate to the other about their dreams.

In attempt to outline and jump-start some important conversations, I've written this book for couples. It's wonderful for partners who are considering getting engaged and married. Surprisingly, it's also useful for married couples who may not have initially discussed things or whose visions and dreams have shifted in the course of their marriage.

This book consists of 100 conversations to have with your partner in twenty major life areas. It is meant to be fun and creative. These conversations culminate in a creative collage that you can both manifest and be inspired by.

I know all the husbands who "hate to talk" will ironically thank me for outlining directives for 100 new conversations with their wives. I say this because I do have a husband of my own. These conversations, however, are not meant to be forums for demands, complaints, or debates. This is an opportunity for you to bring more inspiration, passion, and fun to your relationship by thinking about how you would like it to work and what you are willing to do to attain that vision. The focus and energy of discussion is intended to be positive and the responsibility for your relationship's creation shared.

In my experience, most relational difficulties stem from an inability to communicate about and accept differences. In this book, you will learn how to develop a shared vision that can work for both people involved. I designed it to help couples to develop their communication and visioning skills in their romantic relationship and in all their relationships. It is also somewhat of a diagnostic tool: if you and your partner cannot come to terms on most of the important issues and cannot compromise, it may signal a need for couples counseling to decide whether you should marry and how to fine-tune these skills.

Through love and synergy, we can all create more in our relationships than we could ever do alone. Let your relationship be an example.

Please write and tell me how your journey with this book has transformed your relationship and how your relationship has transformed your life.

My Best in Love,

Paulette

Part I

100 Conversations

Leisure/Fun

♥

1) What do you *love* to do? Will you continue this
activity once you are married?

Her:

_____
_____
_____
_____
_____
_____
_____
_____
_____
_____
_____
_____

Him:

_____
_____
_____
_____

_____
_____
_____
_____
_____
_____
_____
_____
_____

Outcome:

_____
_____
_____
_____
_____
_____
_____

2)   What activities would you like to share with your
      partner?

Her:

_____
_____
_____
_____
_____
_____
_____

_____
_____
_____
_____
_____

Him:

_____
_____
_____
_____
_____
_____
_____
_____
_____
_____
_____

Outcome:

_____
_____
_____
_____
_____
_____
_____

3) What do you like to do in your downtime? Do
    you like to do these activities alone, with friends,
    or with your partner? How much time do you
    need for this?

Her:

_____
_____
_____
_____
_____
_____
_____
_____
_____
_____
_____
_____

Him:

_____
_____
_____
_____
_____
_____
_____
_____
_____

_____
_____
_____
_____

Outcome:

_____
_____
_____
_____
_____
_____

4)   What are the things that you and your partner
      currently do for fun? Are they things you would
      continue after marriage?

Her:

_____
_____
_____
_____
_____
_____
_____
_____
_____
_____
_____

Him:

_____
_____
_____
_____
_____
_____
_____
_____
_____
_____
_____
_____

Outcome:

_____
_____
_____
_____
_____
_____
_____

5)   How much time do you currently allot in your life
     for fun and leisure? Do you take regular
     vacations?

Her:

_____
_____
_____
_____
_____
_____
_____
_____
_____
_____
_____

Him:

_____
_____
_____
_____
_____
_____
_____
_____
_____

_____

_____

_____

Outcome:

_____

_____

_____

_____

_____

_____

_____

Family

♥

6) How close are you to your family?Is there anyone in your family you do not have a good relationship with? If so, why is that relationship strained?

Her:

_____
_____
_____
_____
_____
_____
_____
_____
_____
_____
_____

Him:

_____
_____
_____

_____
_____
_____
_____
_____
_____
_____
_____
_____
_____

Outcome:

_____
_____
_____
_____
_____
_____
_____

7)   How often do you like to see your family of
      origin? How does your fiancé(e) feel about this?

Her:

_____
_____
_____
_____
_____
_____
_____

_____

_____

_____

_____

_____

Him:

_____

_____

_____

_____

_____

_____

_____

_____

_____

_____

_____

_____

Outcome:

_____

_____

_____

_____

_____

_____

8)   How do your fiancé(e) and family of origin get along? If there is tension, have there been efforts made to improve the relationship?

Her:

_____

_____

_____

_____

_____

_____

_____

_____

_____

_____

_____

Him:

_____

_____

_____

_____

_____

_____

_____

_____

_____

_____

_____
_____
_____

Outcome:

9)   What is your most painful memory about your
     family? Why?

Her:

_____
_____
_____
_____
_____
_____
_____
_____
_____
_____
_____

Him:

_____
_____
_____
_____
_____

_____
_____
_____
_____
_____
_____

Outcome:

_____
_____
_____
_____
_____
_____

10)   What is your best family memory and why?

Her:

_____
_____
_____
_____
_____
_____
_____
_____

Him:

_____

_____

_____

_____

_____

_____

_____

_____

_____

_____

_____

_____

_____

Outcome:

_____

_____

_____

_____

_____

_____

_____

Children

♥

11) Do you want kids? If so, how many?

Her:

_____

_____

_____

_____

_____

_____

_____

_____

_____

_____

_____

Him:

_____

_____

_____

_____

_____
_____
_____
_____
_____
_____
_____

Outcome:

_____
_____
_____
_____
_____
_____

12)   When do you want to start having kids? Why is
that a good time frame? Is this negotiable?

Her:

_____
_____
_____
_____
_____
_____
_____

Him:

Outcome:

13)   What would your role be in raising your kids?
      How would your work schedule accommodate
      kids? What would your role as a parent include?

Her:

_____

_____

_____

_____

_____

_____

_____

_____

_____

_____

_____

Him:

_____

_____

_____

_____

_____

_____

_____

_____

_____

_____

_____
_____
_____

Outcome:

_____
_____
_____
_____
_____
_____
_____

14)   In your opinion, what is the most important thing
      about being a good parent?

Her:

_____
_____
_____
_____
_____
_____
_____
_____
_____
_____
_____
_____
_____

Him:

_____
_____
_____
_____
_____
_____
_____
_____
_____
_____
_____
_____

Outcome:

_____
_____
_____
_____
_____
_____
_____

15)   How would you discipline your child?

Her:

_____
_____
_____
_____
_____
_____
_____
_____
_____
_____
_____

Him:

_____
_____
_____
_____
_____
_____
_____
_____
_____

Outcome:

_____

_____

_____

_____

_____

_____

_____

Values

♥

16) How responsible are you? Do your actions
     usually match your words? Give examples:

Her:

_____

_____

_____

_____

_____

_____

_____

_____

_____

_____

Him:

_____

_____

_____

_____

_____

_____

_____

_____

_____

_____

_____

Outcome:

_____

_____

_____

_____

_____

_____

17)   How important is honesty in your relationship?
       Do you tell lies? If so, are they small lies, big lies,
       or somewhere in between? Why do you feel the
       need to lie?

Her:

_____

_____

_____

_____

_____

_____
_____
_____
_____
_____
_____
_____

Him:

_____
_____
_____
_____
_____
_____
_____
_____
_____
_____
_____

Outcome:

_____
_____
_____
_____
_____
_____

18)   What do you value most about marriage (e.g., companionship, trust, love, family, freedom)?

Her:

_____
_____
_____
_____
_____
_____
_____
_____
_____
_____
_____

Him:

_____
_____
_____
_____
_____
_____
_____
_____
_____
_____

Outcome:

_____
_____
_____
_____
_____
_____
_____

19)   What do you value most in your life (e.g.,
      success, education, friends, family, learning)?

Her:

_____
_____
_____
_____
_____
_____
_____
_____
_____
_____
_____
_____
_____

Him:

_____
_____
_____
_____
_____
_____
_____
_____
_____
_____
_____

Outcome:

_____
_____
_____
_____
_____
_____
_____

20)   What do you value most about your fiancé(e)?
Least? What about for yourself?

Her:

_____

_____

_____

_____

_____

_____

_____

_____

_____

_____

_____

Him:

_____

_____

_____

_____

_____

_____

_____

_____

_____

_____

_____

Outcome:

_____

_____

_____

_____

_____

_____

_____

Friends

♥

21) Who are your best friends? Are these close relationships? Have they met your fiancé(e)? How do they get along?

Her:

_____
_____
_____
_____
_____
_____
_____
_____
_____
_____
_____

Him:

_____
_____
_____
_____

_____
_____
_____
_____
_____
_____
_____
_____
_____
_____

Outcome:

_____
_____
_____
_____
_____
_____
_____

22)   How important is it that you continue to see your friends after you are married? Do you want to spend time with them alone or with your spouse and other couples?

Her:

_____
_____
_____
_____
_____

_____
_____
_____
_____
_____
_____
_____
_____

Him:

_____
_____
_____
_____
_____
_____
_____
_____
_____
_____
_____
_____

Outcome:

_____
_____
_____
_____
_____
_____

23)   Do you take weekend outings with your friends?
       How does your fiancé(e) feel about time away?

Her:

_____

_____

_____

_____

_____

_____

_____

_____

_____

_____

_____

Him:

_____

_____

_____

_____

_____

_____

_____

_____

_____

_____

Outcome:

_____

_____

_____

_____

_____

_____

_____

24)   Are there any friends that are a source of distress
      in your relationship? If so, why?

Her:

_____

_____

_____

_____

_____

_____

_____

_____

_____

_____

_____

_____

_____

Him:

_____
_____
_____
_____
_____
_____
_____
_____
_____
_____
_____

Outcome:

_____
_____
_____
_____
_____
_____

25)   Do you each have friends who support your
      relationship?

Her:

_____
_____
_____
_____
_____
_____
_____
_____
_____
_____
_____
_____

Him:

_____
_____
_____
_____
_____
_____
_____
_____
_____
_____
_____

Outcome:

_____

_____

_____

_____

_____

_____

_____

Sex

♥

26) How often would you like to have sex when you are married? Are you liberal or conservative about sexuality?

Her:

_____
_____
_____
_____
_____
_____
_____
_____
_____
_____
_____

Him:

_____
_____
_____
_____

_____
_____
_____
_____
_____
_____
_____
_____
_____
_____

Outcome:

_____
_____
_____
_____
_____
_____

27)   Do you feel comfortable talking about what you want?

Her:

_____
_____
_____
_____
_____
_____

_____
_____
_____
_____
_____

Him:

_____
_____
_____
_____
_____
_____
_____
_____
_____
_____
_____

Outcome:

_____
_____
_____
_____
_____
_____

28)   What might you do to improve your sex life after you have had kids or been married for a while?

Her:

_____
_____
_____
_____
_____
_____
_____
_____
_____
_____
_____

Him:

_____
_____
_____
_____
_____
_____
_____
_____
_____
_____
_____

Outcome:

_____
_____
_____
_____
_____
_____
_____

29)   How do you feel about using birth control in your
      relationship?

Her:

_____
_____
_____
_____
_____
_____
_____
_____
_____
_____
_____
_____

Him:

_____
_____
_____
_____
_____
_____
_____
_____
_____
_____
_____
_____

Outcome:

_____
_____
_____
_____
_____
_____
_____

30)   What are your feelings about abortion should an
      unexpected pregnancy take place? How might
      you communicate with your partner about such
      an event? What would your expectations be?

Her:

_____
_____
_____
_____
_____
_____
_____
_____
_____
_____

Him:

_____
_____
_____
_____
_____
_____
_____

_____

_____

_____

_____

Outcome:

_____

_____

_____

_____

_____

_____

_____

Work/Career

♥

31) Do you love your job? How important is it to you? If you do not like your work, do you plan to change jobs? How does your partner feel about that?

Her:

_____
_____
_____
_____
_____
_____
_____
_____
_____
_____
_____
_____

Him:

_____
_____
_____

_____

_____

_____

_____

_____

_____

_____

_____

_____

_____

_____

Outcome:

_____

_____

_____

_____

_____

_____

32)   Would your work come first in your marriage?
      What type of a balance do you foresee? How
      would you adjust your job for family
      responsibilities?

Her:

_____

_____

_____

_____

_____
_____
_____
_____
_____
_____
_____
_____
_____

Him:

_____
_____
_____
_____
_____
_____
_____
_____
_____
_____
_____
_____

Outcome:

_____
_____
_____
_____
_____

33)   Would you expect your partner to move for your job opportunity? Would you do the same for your partner if the situation were reversed?

Her:

_____

_____

_____

_____

_____

_____

_____

_____

_____

_____

_____

_____

Him:

_____

_____

_____

_____

_____

_____

_____

_____

_____

_____

Outcome:

_____

_____

_____

_____

_____

_____

_____

34)   Do you have goals you want to accomplish in your career? Have you disclosed your goals with your partner and allowed him/her to help you in achieving them?

Her:

_____

_____

_____

_____

_____

_____

_____

_____

_____

_____

_____

_____

Him:

_____
_____
_____
_____
_____
_____
_____
_____
_____
_____
_____
_____

Outcome:

_____
_____
_____
_____
_____
_____

35) When you have retired and look back on your life, do you believe you will have achieved your goals? Are you dissatisfied with your progress on them thus far?

Her:

_____
_____
_____
_____
_____
_____
_____
_____
_____
_____
_____
_____

Him:

_____
_____
_____
_____
_____
_____
_____
_____

_____

_____

_____

_____

Outcome:

_____

_____

_____

_____

_____

_____

_____

Finances

♥

36)   How important is money to you? How much do you make? How much would you like to make?

Her:

_____

_____

_____

_____

_____

_____

_____

_____

_____

_____

Him:

_____

_____

_____

_____
_____
_____
_____
_____
_____
_____
_____

Outcome:

_____
_____
_____
_____
_____
_____
_____

37)   Are you responsible with your money? Is money
      a source of stress for you? Are you in debt? What
      do you need to do to improve your finances?

Her:

_____
_____
_____
_____
_____
_____
_____

_____

_____

_____

_____

_____

_____

Him:

_____

_____

_____

_____

_____

_____

_____

_____

_____

_____

_____

_____

Outcome:

_____

_____

_____

_____

_____

_____

_____

38)   What category of spender do you fall into:
      avoider, spender, or saver? Do you expect your
      partner to adapt to this style?

Her:

_____
_____
_____
_____
_____
_____
_____
_____
_____
_____
_____
_____

Him:

_____
_____
_____
_____
_____
_____
_____
_____
_____
_____
_____

Outcome:

_____
_____
_____
_____
_____
_____
_____

39)   Are you generous or controlling with your
      money?

Her:

_____
_____
_____
_____
_____
_____
_____
_____
_____
_____
_____
_____

Him:

_____

_____

_____

_____

_____

_____

_____

_____

_____

_____

_____

Outcome:

_____

_____

_____

_____

_____

_____

40) Do you have a system for money? Does it differ from your partner's? How might you develop a system together?

Her:

_____

_____

_____

_____

_____

_____

_____

_____

_____

_____

_____

Him:

_____

_____

_____

_____

_____

_____

_____

_____

_____

_____

Outcome:

_____

_____

_____

_____

_____

_____

_____

Personal Development

♥

41) What dreams do you have? Have you told them to your partner? Do you let them help you to achieve them?

Her:

_____
_____
_____
_____
_____
_____
_____
_____
_____
_____
_____

Him:

_____
_____
_____
_____

_____
_____
_____
_____
_____
_____
_____
_____
_____

Outcome:

_____
_____
_____
_____
_____
_____

42)   What do you still want to learn in your life (e.g.,
      piano, travel, karate, dancing)?

Her:

_____
_____
_____
_____
_____
_____

_____
_____
_____
_____
_____

Him:

_____
_____
_____
_____
_____
_____
_____
_____
_____
_____
_____
_____

Outcome:

_____
_____
_____
_____
_____
_____
_____

43)   What do you need from your partner in order to
      grow emotionally and spiritually? Do you get it?

Her:

_____

_____

_____

_____

_____

_____

_____

_____

_____

_____

_____

_____

Him:

_____

_____

_____

_____

_____

_____

_____

_____

_____

_____

_____

_____

Outcome:

_____
_____
_____
_____
_____
_____
_____

44) Where do you see yourself in five years in all
     areas of your life? How does your partner fit into
     this picture?

Her:

_____
_____
_____
_____
_____
_____
_____
_____
_____
_____
_____
_____
_____

Him:

_____
_____
_____
_____
_____
_____
_____
_____
_____
_____
_____
_____

Outcome:

_____
_____
_____
_____
_____
_____
_____
_____

45) Do you have goals to develop yourself in the context of your relationship? What ways would you like to grow there?

Her:

_____
_____
_____
_____
_____
_____
_____
_____
_____
_____
_____
_____

Him:

_____
_____
_____
_____
_____
_____
_____
_____
_____
_____

_____

_____

Outcome:

_____

_____

_____

_____

_____

_____

_____

Spirituality/Religion

♥

46) Do you believe in God? What is your conception of God in your life?

Her:

_____

_____

_____

_____

_____

_____

_____

_____

_____

_____

Him:

_____

_____

_____

_____

_____
_____
_____
_____
_____
_____
_____
_____

Outcome:

_____
_____
_____
_____
_____
_____

47)   What was your religious experience growing up?
       Is this different from your partner's experience?
       Does this bother you? Can you learn from your
       partner's experience? How do you feel about
       participating in your religion?

Her:

_____
_____
_____
_____
_____

_____
_____
_____
_____
_____
_____
_____
_____

Him:

_____
_____
_____
_____
_____
_____
_____
_____
_____
_____
_____

Outcome:

_____
_____
_____
_____
_____
_____

48)   What role will religion play in your new family life?

Her:

_____

_____

_____

_____

_____

_____

_____

_____

_____

_____

_____

Him:

_____

_____

_____

_____

_____

_____

_____

_____

_____

_____

Outcome:

_____

_____

_____

_____

_____

_____

_____

49)   Will your kids celebrate religious holidays or go
      to a religious school?

Her:

_____

_____

_____

_____

_____

_____

_____

_____

_____

_____

_____

_____

Him:

_____
_____
_____
_____
_____
_____
_____
_____
_____
_____
_____
_____

Outcome:

_____
_____
_____
_____
_____
_____
_____

50)   What does spirituality mean to you? How do you
      honor it in your own way? What do you want to
      create around spirituality in your life?

Her:

_____
_____
_____
_____
_____
_____
_____
_____
_____
_____
_____
_____

Him:

_____
_____
_____
_____
_____
_____
_____
_____
_____
_____

Outcome:

_____

_____

_____

_____

_____

_____

_____

Ethnicity

♥

51) What is your ethnic heritage? Have you been to
the country where your ancestors lived? What
stories have you heard about this? What traditions
do you want to include in your new family?

Her:

_____
_____
_____
_____
_____
_____
_____
_____
_____
_____
_____
_____
_____

Him:

_____

_____

_____

_____

_____

_____

_____

_____

_____

_____

_____

_____

_____

Outcome:

_____

_____

_____

_____

_____

_____

_____

_____

52)   How does your heritage affect you now?

Her:

_____
_____
_____
_____
_____
_____
_____
_____
_____
_____
_____

Him:

_____
_____
_____
_____
_____
_____
_____
_____
_____
_____
_____

Outcome:

_____
_____
_____
_____
_____
_____
_____

53)   Will your heritage be important in raising your
        kids?

Her:

_____
_____
_____
_____
_____
_____
_____
_____
_____
_____
_____
_____

Him:

_____
_____
_____
_____
_____
_____
_____
_____
_____
_____
_____
_____

Outcome:

_____
_____
_____
_____
_____
_____
_____

54)   Does this conflict with your partner's cultural
       heritage? Have you discussed this?

Her:

_____

_____

_____

_____

_____

_____

_____

_____

_____

_____

_____

Him:

_____

_____

_____

_____

_____

_____

_____

_____

_____

_____

_____

Outcome:

_____
_____
_____
_____
_____
_____
_____

55)   Do your extended families have an understanding
      of your shared cultural vision? If not, how will
      you deal with this?

Her:

_____
_____
_____
_____
_____
_____
_____
_____
_____
_____
_____
_____
_____

Him:

_____
_____
_____
_____
_____
_____
_____
_____
_____
_____
_____
_____

Outcome:

_____
_____
_____
_____
_____
_____
_____

56)   How will you expose your kids to both cultures?

Her:

_____
_____
_____
_____
_____
_____
_____
_____
_____
_____
_____

Him:

_____
_____
_____
_____
_____
_____
_____
_____
_____
_____
_____

Outcome:

_____

_____

_____

_____

_____

_____

_____

Preferences

♥

57)   What is your favorite way to celebrate something good in your life?

Her:

_____
_____
_____
_____
_____
_____
_____
_____
_____
_____

Him:

_____
_____
_____
_____

_____
_____
_____
_____
_____
_____
_____
_____

Outcome:

_____
_____
_____
_____
_____
_____

58)   Are you a morning or an evening person? How will this affect your relationship with your partner?

Her:

_____
_____
_____
_____
_____
_____
_____

_____
_____
_____
_____

Him:

_____
_____
_____
_____
_____
_____
_____
_____
_____
_____
_____
_____

Outcome:

_____
_____
_____
_____
_____
_____
_____

59)   Do you like to be one-on-one with people or do
      you prefer groups? Is this very different from
      your partner?

Her:

_____
_____
_____
_____
_____
_____
_____
_____
_____
_____
_____

Him:

_____
_____
_____
_____
_____
_____
_____
_____
_____
_____

Outcome:

_____

_____

_____

_____

_____

_____

60)   What is your favorite type of vacation and where would it be?

Her:

_____

_____

_____

_____

_____

_____

_____

_____

_____

_____

Him:

_____
_____
_____
_____
_____
_____
_____
_____
_____
_____
_____
_____

Outcome:

_____
_____
_____
_____
_____
_____
_____

61)   What is the best gift your partner could give you?

Her:

_____
_____
_____
_____
_____
_____
_____
_____
_____
_____
_____

Him:

_____
_____
_____
_____
_____
_____
_____
_____
_____
_____
_____

Outcome:

_____

_____

_____

_____

_____

_____

_____

Environment

♥

62)   What kind of house or apartment do you want?

Her:

_____

_____

_____

_____

_____

_____

_____

_____

_____

_____

_____

_____

Him:

_____

_____

_____

_____

_____

_____

_____

_____

_____

_____

_____

_____

Outcome:

_____

_____

_____

_____

_____

_____

63)   What climate or location would you most like to live in? Do you need nature? Mountains? The beach? Do you prefer the city? Neighbors? Privacy?

Her:

_____

_____

_____

_____

_____

_____

_____
_____
_____
_____
_____
_____

Him:

_____
_____
_____
_____
_____
_____
_____
_____
_____
_____
_____
_____

Outcome:

_____
_____
_____
_____
_____
_____

64)   Are you neat or messy? Would you get a maid?
      What responsibility will you have for household
      duties?

Her:

_____
_____
_____
_____
_____
_____
_____
_____
_____
_____
_____

Him:

_____
_____
_____
_____
_____
_____
_____
_____
_____
_____
_____

Outcome:

_____
_____
_____
_____
_____
_____
_____

65)   How do you decorate? Do you need or want an
      active role in this? Are you romantic, creative,
      conservative, minimalist, or utilitarian?

Her:

_____
_____
_____
_____
_____
_____
_____
_____
_____
_____
_____
_____

Him:

_____
_____
_____
_____
_____
_____
_____
_____
_____
_____
_____
_____
_____
_____

Outcome:

_____
_____
_____
_____
_____
_____
_____

66)   Do you need your own space, like an office or
      sanctuary?

Her:

_____

_____

_____

_____

_____

_____

_____

_____

_____

_____

_____

_____

Him:

_____

_____

_____

_____

_____

_____

_____

_____

_____

_____

_____

Outcome:

_____
_____
_____
_____
_____
_____
_____

67)   In what kind of environment did you grow up?
      What would you like to replicate or change for
      your new family?

Her:

_____
_____
_____
_____
_____
_____
_____
_____
_____
_____
_____
_____

Him:

_____
_____
_____
_____
_____
_____
_____
_____
_____
_____
_____
_____
_____

Outcome:

_____
_____
_____
_____
_____
_____
_____

Marital Vision

♥

68) What was your idea about marriage as a child? Has it changed?

Her:

_____

_____

_____

_____

_____

_____

_____

_____

_____

_____

_____

Him:

_____

_____

_____

_____

_____
_____
_____
_____
_____
_____
_____
_____

Outcome:

_____
_____
_____
_____
_____
_____

69)   What appeals to you the most about marriage?
       What appeals to you the least?

Her:

_____
_____
_____
_____
_____
_____
_____

_____

_____

_____

_____

Him:

_____

_____

_____

_____

_____

_____

_____

_____

_____

_____

_____

_____

Outcome:

_____

_____

_____

_____

_____

_____

_____

_____

_____

70)   What scares you the most about getting married?
        Discuss this with your partner.

Her:

_____
_____
_____
_____
_____
_____
_____
_____
_____
_____
_____
_____

Him:

_____
_____
_____
_____
_____
_____
_____
_____
_____
_____
_____

Outcome:

_____
_____
_____
_____
_____
_____
_____

71)   What kind of marriage did your parents have? Do
      you possess the same dynamic in your current
      relationship?

Her:

_____
_____
_____
_____
_____
_____
_____
_____
_____
_____
_____
_____

Him:

_____
_____
_____
_____
_____
_____
_____
_____
_____
_____
_____
_____
_____

Outcome:

_____
_____
_____
_____
_____
_____
_____

72)   What vision do you currently want to create by
      marrying your partner?

Her:

_____
_____
_____
_____
_____
_____
_____
_____
_____
_____
_____
_____

Him:

_____
_____
_____
_____
_____
_____
_____
_____
_____
_____
_____

Outcome:

_____
_____
_____
_____
_____
_____

73)   How would you feel about divorce, should your
      vision not be realized? How flexible would you
      be? How much stress do you feel a marriage
      should be able to take?

Her:

_____
_____
_____
_____
_____
_____
_____
_____
_____
_____
_____
_____

Him:

_____
_____
_____
_____
_____
_____
_____
_____
_____
_____
_____
_____
_____

Outcome:

_____
_____
_____
_____
_____
_____
_____
_____

Stress/Crisis

♥

74) How do you respond in a crisis? Do you get involved, pull away and avoid it, talk it out, consult friends, et cetera?

Her:

_____
_____
_____
_____
_____
_____
_____
_____
_____
_____
_____
_____

Him:

_____
_____
_____
_____

_____

_____

_____

_____

_____

_____

_____

_____

_____

_____

_____

Outcome:

_____

_____

_____

_____

_____

_____

_____

_____

75)   How do you deal with your anger and disappointment in your relationships? Do you yell, become violent, walk away, shut down, talk it out, problem solve, et cetera?

Her:

_____
_____
_____
_____
_____
_____
_____
_____
_____
_____
_____
_____
_____

Him:

_____
_____
_____
_____
_____
_____
_____
_____

_____
_____
_____
_____

Outcome:

_____
_____
_____
_____
_____
_____
_____

76)   Describe one crisis you have already dealt with together. How did you do?

Her:

_____
_____
_____
_____
_____
_____
_____
_____
_____
_____

Him:

_____
_____
_____
_____
_____
_____
_____
_____
_____
_____
_____
_____
_____
_____

Outcome:

_____
_____
_____
_____
_____
_____
_____
_____

77)   Describe one crisis you have dealt with outside of your relationship. How did you deal with it? What did you learn?

Her:

_____
_____
_____
_____
_____
_____
_____
_____
_____
_____
_____

Him:

_____
_____
_____
_____
_____
_____
_____
_____

_____
_____
_____
_____

Outcome:

_____
_____
_____
_____
_____
_____
_____

78)   Given that stress in your marriage is expectable,
      what will you do when that stress seems too
      much?

Her:

_____
_____
_____
_____
_____
_____
_____
_____
_____
_____
_____
_____
_____

Him:

_____
_____
_____
_____
_____
_____
_____
_____
_____
_____
_____
_____

Outcome:

_____
_____
_____
_____
_____
_____
_____

Differences

♥

79) What differences exist between you and your partner? What is attractive about this? What bothers you?

Her:

_____

_____

_____

_____

_____

_____

_____

_____

_____

_____

_____

_____

Him:

_____

_____

_____

_____

_____
_____
_____
_____
_____
_____
_____
_____
_____
_____
_____

Outcome:

_____
_____
_____
_____
_____
_____
_____

80) Have you been able to implement outside-of–the-box solutions to make these differences work in your relationship?

Her:

_____
_____
_____
_____
_____
_____

_____
_____
_____
_____
_____
_____

Him:

_____
_____
_____
_____
_____
_____
_____
_____
_____
_____
_____
_____

Outcome:

_____
_____
_____
_____
_____
_____
_____

81) What can you learn from your partner's differences?

Her:

_____

_____

_____

_____

_____

_____

_____

_____

_____

_____

_____

Him:

_____

_____

_____

_____

_____

_____

_____

_____

_____

_____

_____

Outcome:

_____

_____

_____

_____

_____

_____

82)   Do you feel your partner accepts you? Does
       he/she want to change you in certain ways? Do
       you like those things he/she wants to change
       about yourself?

Her:

_____

_____

_____

_____

_____

_____

_____

_____

_____

_____

_____

_____

Him:

_____
_____
_____
_____
_____
_____
_____
_____
_____
_____
_____
_____
_____

Outcome:

_____
_____
_____
_____
_____
_____
_____
_____

83)   What would you most like to change about the
      other person and about yourself?

Her:

_____
_____
_____
_____
_____
_____
_____
_____
_____
_____
_____
_____

Him:

_____
_____
_____
_____
_____
_____
_____
_____
_____
_____
_____
_____

Outcome:

_____
_____
_____
_____
_____
_____
_____

84)   Are the prejudices and judgments you have about
      your differences with your partner yours or were
      they old patterns and limiting beliefs inherited
      from your parents?

Her:

_____
_____
_____
_____
_____
_____
_____
_____
_____
_____
_____
_____

Him:

_____
_____
_____
_____
_____
_____
_____
_____
_____
_____
_____
_____
_____

Outcome:

_____
_____
_____
_____
_____
_____
_____

Space

♥

85) How much emotional and physical space do you need? How much time would you like to talk to and see your partner?

Her:

_____
_____
_____
_____
_____
_____
_____
_____
_____
_____
_____
_____

Him:

_____
_____
_____
_____

_____
_____
_____
_____
_____
_____
_____
_____
_____
_____

Outcome:

_____
_____
_____
_____
_____
_____

86)   Are your relationships with family members
      close? Do you discuss your feelings? Do you
      discuss feelings openly with your partner?

Her:

_____
_____
_____
_____
_____

_____
_____
_____
_____
_____
_____

Him:

_____
_____
_____
_____
_____
_____
_____
_____
_____
_____
_____
_____
_____

Outcome:

_____
_____
_____
_____
_____
_____
_____

87) How much freedom do you need in your relationship to make independent choices? How is this negotiated in your relationship now? Give an example:

Her:

_____
_____
_____
_____
_____
_____
_____
_____
_____
_____
_____
_____
_____

Him:

_____
_____
_____
_____
_____
_____
_____
_____

_____

_____

_____

_____

Outcome:

_____

_____

_____

_____

_____

_____

88)   Are you able to tell your partner when you need
       space? Is he/she supportive in making provisions
       for this?

Her:

_____

_____

_____

_____

_____

_____

_____

_____

_____

Him:

_____
_____
_____
_____
_____
_____
_____
_____
_____
_____
_____
_____

Outcome:

_____
_____
_____
_____
_____
_____
_____

Wedding Vision

♥

89) Describe the wedding of your dreams. Think about the location, meaning, number of people, money, vows, et cetera.

Her:

_____
_____
_____
_____
_____
_____
_____
_____
_____
_____
_____

Him:

_____
_____
_____

_____
_____
_____
_____
_____
_____
_____
_____
_____
_____
_____

Outcome:

_____
_____
_____
_____
_____
_____

90) How important is it to you to be involved in
     planning the wedding?

Her:

_____
_____
_____
_____
_____
_____
_____

_____
_____
_____
_____
_____

Him:

_____
_____
_____
_____
_____
_____
_____
_____
_____
_____
_____
_____

Outcome:

_____
_____
_____
_____
_____
_____
_____
_____

91)   How will marriage change your relationship?
      How will it get better? How might it get worse?

Her:

_____
_____
_____
_____
_____
_____
_____
_____
_____
_____
_____
_____

Him:

_____
_____
_____
_____
_____
_____
_____
_____
_____
_____
_____
_____

Outcome:

_____

_____

_____

_____

_____

_____

_____

92)   How will marriage affect the other areas of your life?

Her:

_____

_____

_____

_____

_____

_____

_____

_____

_____

_____

_____

_____

_____

Him:

_____
_____
_____
_____
_____
_____
_____
_____
_____
_____
_____
_____

Outcome:

_____
_____
_____
_____
_____
_____
_____

Retirement

♥

93)   How do you picture your retirement?

Her:

_____
_____
_____
_____
_____
_____
_____
_____
_____
_____
_____
_____

Him:

_____
_____
_____
_____
_____

_____
_____
_____
_____
_____
_____
_____
_____

Outcome:

_____
_____
_____
_____
_____
_____
_____

94)   What do you hope to have accomplished by the
      time you are eighty years old? What do you want
      your legacy to be? How will your partner help
      you with that?

Her:

_____
_____
_____
_____
_____
_____

_____
_____
_____
_____
_____
_____

Him:

_____
_____
_____
_____
_____
_____
_____
_____
_____
_____
_____
_____

Outcome:

_____
_____
_____
_____
_____
_____

95)   Do you have a retirement plan and long-term
      financial goal?

Her:

_____

_____

_____

_____

_____

_____

_____

_____

_____

_____

_____

Him:

_____

_____

_____

_____

_____

_____

_____

_____

_____

_____

Outcome:

_____
_____
_____
_____
_____
_____
_____

96)   How would you react if your partner became
       disabled and you had to take care of his/her
       physical needs?

Her:

_____
_____
_____
_____
_____
_____
_____
_____
_____
_____
_____
_____
_____
_____

Him:

_____
_____
_____
_____
_____
_____
_____
_____
_____
_____
_____
_____
_____

Outcome:

_____
_____
_____
_____
_____
_____

Romance

♥

97) What makes you feel most loved and cherished?
     What would you like your partner to do to
     romance you even more?

Her:

_____
_____
_____
_____
_____
_____
_____
_____
_____
_____
_____
_____

Him:

_____
_____
_____
_____

_____
_____
_____
_____
_____
_____
_____
_____
_____
_____

Outcome:

_____
_____
_____
_____
_____
_____

98)   What is your most romantic memory with your
      partner and why?

Her:

_____
_____
_____
_____
_____
_____

_____
_____
_____
_____
_____

Him:

_____
_____
_____
_____
_____
_____
_____
_____
_____
_____
_____
_____

Outcome:

_____
_____
_____
_____
_____
_____
_____

99)   What do you do that your partner considers romantic? What does your partner do that you consider romantic?

Her:

_____
_____
_____
_____
_____
_____
_____
_____
_____
_____
_____

Him:

_____
_____
_____
_____
_____
_____
_____
_____
_____
_____

Outcome:

_____

_____

_____

_____

_____

_____

_____

100)   What romantic things can you do as a couple to
       sustain your relationship over time?

Her:

_____

_____

_____

_____

_____

_____

_____

_____

_____

_____

_____

_____

Him:

_____

_____

_____

_____

_____

_____

_____

_____

_____

_____

_____

_____

_____

Outcome:

_____

_____

_____

_____

_____

_____

_____

Part II

Challenging Areas

Look at all the items you have read and discussed. Particularly review those items that presented some conflict. Item by item, review where you and your partner have differing views on certain issues. How can you address them together as a team?

a) Brainstorm at least seven solutions to each of the questions where your views are different. Do not judge the possibilities. Can you use your goodwill and synergy to create something together that is better than you would create alone?

_____

_____

_____

_____

_____

_____

_____

_____

_____

_____

_____

_____

_____

_____

_____

_____

b) If you cannot come up with a shared vision for an item, rate the importance of that item to you. Is it more important to you or to your partner? Is it something you would be willing to compromise for the sake of your relationship?

_____

_____

_____

_____

_____

_____

_____

_____

_____

_____

_____

_____

_____

_____

_____

_____

c) Are you still stuck on an issue? If so, put a star next to it and move on. You can come back to it later when you do an overall appraisal of your relationship.

Record Challenging Issues Here:

Stuck Issue No. 1:

Possible Solutions:

_____

_____

_____

_____

_____

_____

_____

_____

_____

_____

_____

_____

_____

_____

_____

_____

_____

_____

_____

_____

_____

_____

_____

Level of Importance (0–10)
Him=___ Her=___

Decision Reached:

_____
_____
_____
_____
_____

Stuck Issue No. 2:

Possible Solutions:

_____
_____
_____
_____
_____
_____
_____
_____
_____
_____
_____
_____
_____
_____
_____
_____

_____

_____

_____

_____

_____

Level of Importance (0–10)
Him=___ Her=___

Decision Reached:

_____

_____

_____

_____

_____

Stuck Issue No. 3:

Possible Solutions:

_____

_____

_____

_____

_____

_____

_____

_____

_____

_____

_____
_____
_____
_____
_____
_____
_____
_____

Level of Importance (0–10)
Him=___ Her=___

Decision Reached:

_____
_____
_____
_____

Stuck Issue No. 4:

Possible Solutions:

_____
_____
_____
_____
_____

_____

_____

_____

_____

_____

_____

_____

_____

_____

_____

_____

_____

_____

_____

Level of Importance (0–10)
Him=___ Her=___

Decision Reached:

_____

_____

_____

_____

_____

Stuck Issue No. 5:

Possible Solutions:

_____

_____

_____

_____

_____

_____

_____

_____

_____

_____

_____

_____

_____

_____

_____

_____

_____

_____

_____

_____

_____

_____

_____

Level of Importance (0–10)
Him=___ Her=___

Decision Reached:

_____
_____
_____
_____

Stuck Issue No. 6:

Possible Solutions:

_____
_____
_____
_____
_____
_____
_____
_____
_____
_____
_____
_____
_____
_____
_____
_____

_____
_____
_____
_____
_____
_____
_____
_____

Level of Importance (0–10)
Him=___ Her=___

Decision Reached:

_____
_____
_____
_____

Stuck Issue No. 7:

Possible Solutions:

_____
_____
_____
_____
_____
_____
_____
_____

_____
_____
_____
_____
_____
_____
_____
_____
_____
_____
_____
_____
_____

Level of Importance (0–10)
Him=___ Her=___

Decision Reached:

_____
_____
_____
_____
_____

Stuck Issue No. 8:

Possible Solutions:

_____
_____
_____

_____

_____

_____

_____

_____

_____

_____

_____

_____

_____

_____

_____

_____

_____

_____

_____

_____

_____

_____

_____

_____

Level of Importance (0–10)
Him=___ Her=___

Decision Reached:

_____

_____

_____

_____

Stuck Issue No. 9:

Possible Solutions:

_____
_____
_____
_____
_____
_____
_____
_____
_____
_____
_____
_____
_____
_____
_____
_____
_____
_____
_____
_____
_____

Level of Importance (0–10)
Him=___ Her=___

Decision Reached:

_____
_____
_____
_____
_____

Stuck Issue No. 10:

Possible Solutions:

_____
_____
_____
_____
_____
_____
_____
_____
_____
_____
_____
_____
_____
_____
_____
_____

_____
_____
_____
_____
_____
_____
_____

Level of Importance (0–10)
Him=___ Her=___

Decision Reached:

_____
_____
_____
_____
_____

Part III

A Shared Vision

Look at all 100 of the outcome paragraphs for the 20 categories that you have discussed. Take some time to review them now and then create a beautiful Shared Vision for your life together. The categories are listed below to jog your memory:

Leisure/Fun

Family

Kids

Values

Sex

Friends

Work/Career

Finances

Personal Development

Spirituality/Religion

Ethnicity

Preferences

Environment

Marital Vision

Crisis/Stress

Differences

Space

Wedding Vision

Retirement

Romance

Other

Exercise No. 1: A Shared Vision Collage

Congratulations! You should be very proud of yourselves. You have done your vision work and chosen the template for your dream relationship. You have put it into words and recorded your blueprint. Now, I want you to make it visual.

What you'll need for this project:

- A pile of magazines
- 2 pairs of scissors
- A bunch of glue sticks
- A big poster board
- Some paints, crayons, or markers

Instructions:

1. Rent some movies about love and grab a pile of old magazines. Both of you cut out pictures that inspire you and that remind you of the dream relationship that you've discussed. Do not discuss it or over think it at this point. Let your heart and subconscious do the choosing and just make a large stack of cut-out images.

2. Then turn off the movies and spend some time together while you glue pictures on a collage. Do not strive for perfection or argue. This is meant to be fun, a type of play. Whatever you create together is great.

3. After you have glued the pictures on, draw words or paint colors on the collage to intensify the feelings and values you hope to create together.

You can create this collage in steps if you do not have a lot of time. Do one step per day. When it is completed, frame your Shared Vision and hang it above your bed. Your subconscious mind responds to imagery, so it will work with you both to manifest your creation. You will be surprised to see that some of the things you have included in the collage will manifest in your relationship automatically.

Here is an example of a Shared Vision:

A Shared Vision Collage

Feel free to send me a copy of yours!
(e-mail: kpaulet@verizon.net)

Exercise No. 2: Action Steps

You can also consciously create your Shared Vision through action steps. For example, if you are a Jewish woman engaged to a Christian man and you've decided that you want to raise your children in the Unitarian Church, why don't you visit a few and see how you feel? You can begin to lay the groundwork for your vision in this area.

If you dream of spending a month in Europe together, buy a guidebook and research where you'd want to go. Find out approximately how much the flights and hotels would cost. Then you can create a savings account and save what you can every month toward that shared goal. Every time you get unexpected money, you'll now know where to put it.

Often, when you are clear about your goals, it becomes easy to take baby steps to achieve it. You just have to be on the same page as your partner and direct your energy toward the same outcome.

I know that you will create a beautiful life together. If this journey has taught you to create as a team, you will always be an empowered couple. You can change your vision at any time and go back to the drawing board. Great couples always reinvent their relationship. The process is just as fun as the results.

Enjoy!

Afterword

Congratulations on your journey as a couple. A Shared Vision creates a road map and marks your intention to walk through life together in the same direction and on the same path. Marriage and a long-term, committed relationship will invite unexpected twists and turns no matter how much you plan, but developing skills for communication, negotiation, and a joint vision will serve you no matter what happens along the way. Remember to love and cherish each other and to really enjoy your journey together!

My Best in Love,

Paulette
www.mydatingschool.com

About the Author

Dr. Paulette Kouffman Sherman is a licensed psychologist, owner of My Dating School (www.mydatingschool.com), author of Dating from the Inside Out, published by Atria Books and When Mars Women Date, published by Parachute Jump Publishing and many other relationship books. She is a regular speaker at The Learning Annex and the NY Love Examiner. She's been an expert on television like the CBS Early Show & the AM Northwest Early Show and a radio guest on the Curtis Sliwa show. She's been quoted on MSN.com, USA Weekend, the NY Post, Newsweek, Lifetime.com, More, Match.com, Foxnews.com, Fox Business, Better Homes & Gardens, Reader's Digest, Redbook, Glamour, Forbes, Woman's Day, Metro newspapers, Men's Health, Seventeen, Complete Woman magazines, and the NY Times. Her new book, *When Mars Women Date: How Career Women Can Love Themselves into the Relationship of their Dreams* can be ordered as an ebook on Amazon through October. It will come out in the print version in December 2012. Learn more on her website: www.whenmarswomendate.com and www.parachutejumppublishing.com!

If you like what you just read
and want to learn more . . .

OTHER BOOKS BY
DR. PAULETTE KOUFFMAN SHERMAN

Dating from the Inside Out:
How to Use the Law of Attraction in Matters of the Heart

A Shared Vision:
100 Conversations to Co-Create the Relationship of Your Dreams

100 Ways to Treat Your Mate like Royalty:
Under $10

When Mars Women Date:
How Career Women Can Love Themselves Into
The Relationship Of Their Dreams

You can also visit Dr. Paulette Kouffman Sherman's website, *My Dating School*, for information on dating coaching. Attend her seminars, order her other books, or invite her to speak at your venue. She will be holding webinars, teleclasses, live groups, and individual coaching sessions for the Mars Woman. Please do contact her at www.whenmarswomendate.com and www.parachutejumppublishing if you are interested in participating or sending her your thoughts on this book.

See you there!

Paulette

http://www.parachutejumppublishing.com
http://www.whenmarswomendate.com
http://www.mydatingschool.com

Made in the USA
Lexington, KY
04 April 2015